AROUND
TETTENHALL
AND
CODSALL
IN OLD PHOTOGRAPHS

COLLECTED BY
MARY MILLS

ALAN SUTTON

Alan Sutton Publishing Limited
Phoenix Mill · Far Thrupp · Stroud · Gloucestershire

First published 1990

British Library Cataloguing in Publication Data

Around Tettenhall and Codsall in old photographs.
1. Staffordshire, history   2. West Midlands (Metropolitan County)
I. Mills, Mary *1949–*
942.46

ISBN 0-86299-760-7

Typeset in 9/10 Korinna.
Typesetting and origination by
Alan Sutton Publishing Limited.
Printed in Great Britain by
Dotesios Printers Limited.

AROUND
TETTENHALL
AND
CODSALL
IN OLD PHOTOGRAPHS

TETTENHALL UDC STEAMROLLER pictured in Long Lake Avenue.

CONTENTS

INTRODUCTION

The area covered by this volume encompasses the two parishes of Codsall and Tettenhall which lie to the west of the town of Wolverhampton, on the western boundary of the county of Staffordshire. The main centres of population in these parishes today are Tettenhall, Tettenhall Wood, Compton, Wightwick, Codsall, Bilbrook, Perton and Pendeford. Smaller centres include Oaken, Kingswood and Codsall Wood.

The nature of the area has changed from that of a largely rural and sparsely populated region of small villages and large country estates to one of suburban communities, commuter villages and new housing estates.

Tettenhall is an ancient village. The earliest mention of the name dates back to 910 when it is recorded as the site of a battle between the Saxons and the Danes. By the time of the Domesday survey in 1086 Tettenhall had a church and population of forty-eight.

In 1894 the Urban District of Tettenhall was formed. The population rose sharply from the 1870s reaching 5,337 in 1901 and 14,867 by 1951. In 1966, despite local opposition, most of the built-up parts of the district became part of Wolverhampton Borough.

Tettenhall has never been an industrial area although in the early days of the nineteenth century the cottage industries of buckle making, lock making and spectacle frame making, 'gave employment to many of the village workmen who sold their wares to the large masters and merchants of Wolverhampton'. This quotation is taken from a history of Tettenhall written in 1894 by James P. Jones who described Tettenhall at that date as 'rapidly becoming a residential suburb of Wolverhampton'. Even in 1850 Kelly's Directory described Tettenhall as 'a pleasant place [which] is chiefly occupied by gentry and the merchants and traders of Wolverhampton.'

As well as providing a pleasant environment close to the towns of the Black Country Tettenhall has also had good communications from an early date. A main coaching route, the Holyhead Road passed right through the centre of the village via Old Hill and Wrottesley Road and later by way of Tettenhall Rock and the Wergs road. Tram and later trolleybus routes served the area well from the later years of the nineteenth century with the best horses and newest vehicles used on this prestigious route. Special workmen's cars were run to take commuters into the town from 1901. The railway came in 1925 connecting Tettenhall to Wolverhampton and Kingswinford.

The area around Tettenhall Wood was originally known as Kingsley Wood and formed part of the parish of Kinver. According to Jones's history its common was the haunt of gypsies, thieves and other disreputable people. The village grew up around the top of the Holloway and Ormes Lane. In White's Directory of 1851 Tettenhall Wood was described thus: 'Several handsome houses and a great number of cottages have been built ... also a small Methodist chapel – the cottages are mostly occupied by lock makers.'

There were many large houses and estates in the early part of the twentieth century and a number of village people were employed in these establishments, often living in houses provided by their employers. Since the Second World War most of these houses have been either demolished or converted to other uses and small residential developments have been built. Council estates were built on either side of School Road soon after the war.

The population increased greatly in the 1950s and, since then, the settlements of Tettenhall and Tettenhall Wood have merged but the two communities still retain very different identities for the people who live there.

Compton was described in 1850 as 'a neat village, two miles west of Wolverhampton where a considerable quantity of red sand is got for the use of iron founders and mixing with mortar.' The building of the Staffordshire and Worcestershire canal was an important event for Compton. The canal was built in 1766 by James Brindley and the section from Compton to Newbridge was the first stretch to be cut, along the valley of the Smestow.

However, Compton, like Tettenhall, developed largely into a residential area for Wolverhampton with the building of several large villas in the late nineteenth century. Again only a few of these now survive, mainly occupied by institutions, and the area is one of small private housing developments.

There was a hall at Wightwick owned by the Wightwick family in the thirteenth century or possibly earlier. Wightwick Hall and the land around it was bought by Theodore Mander, a local industrialist and mayor of Wolverhampton, in 1887. He built Wightwick Manor and restyled Wightwick Hall as well as building some houses in the same style on the Bridgnorth Road.

The original settlement at Perton lay round a village green. In 1086 it was the largest settlement in the area but both village and hall have now disappeared. Recent development has followed the line of Tinacre Hill and Pattingham Road. During World War Two land at Perton was used as an airfield while part of the adjoining Wrottesley estate was occupied by Dutch troops. The former airfield was owned by the Mander family and was sold in 1960 for building. A large modern housing estate has since been built.

Kingswood Common has long been used by Wolverhampton people for recreation and is still a popular picnic place. The area is well known to generations of schoolchildren from the town due to the Kingswood camp which was used by the education committee to give pupils a break in the countryside and lessons in nature study. In 1942 a school was established at the camp for delicate pupils who would benefit from lessons and activities in the open air plus good food and medical supervision.

Part of Kingswood lies in Codsall parish along with Oaken and Codsall Wood, with Codsall itself by far the largest of these places.

Codsall Wood was originally an area of waste and was inhabited by the fourteenth century, housing several families by the seventeenth century. People from Wolverhampton and the Black Country used to visit the area at weekends and tea rooms were provided by the early 1900s. In earlier times Codsall Wood was visited as a spa for people to drink water from a nearby sulphur well which was believed to cure many ailments including leprosy. Agriculture has always been the main industry although sand was dug in the area.

Oaken lies in the south of the parish and is a very ancient township. In 1841 there were only three families and it remained a small hamlet although several large houses were built nearby. The land belonged to the Wrottesley estate whose workers were housed in some of the cottages.

Codsall is not as old a settlement as Oaken although the Domesday book recorded six people living there. The original village grew up around the church and along Church Road. From the 1840s Codsall became largely a residential village for people who worked in Wolverhampton and after the railway was opened in 1850 people who worked in the Black Country also came here to live. Codsall's good communications also encouraged industrialists to move into the area and build large houses or villas. Some, like the Gaskell family, bought existing country estates and carried out various improvements to the land and buildings. The population rose steadily during the first half of the twentieth century but remained under 3,000 until the 1950s when large housing estates were built and the numbers rose rapidly. There has been little industry in the area apart from sandstone quarrying at several sites including Chapel Lane, formerly Quarry Lane. There are many sandstone walls in the area and both Codsall and Tettenhall church were built with Codsall stone. Most people worked in agriculture and the proximity to large Midland towns led to the establishment of nurseries and market gardening.

In the 1880s a newspaper feature described Codsall as '. . . a place where teas are to be had at ninepence a head . . . just far enough from Wolverhampton to offer an excuse for a walk . . . amongst places one ought to visit when rambling through the Midlands.' Day trips were popular up to the 1930s.

Bilbrook was only a small, rather scattered, village until the 1930s when the Lane Green estate was built to house workers at the Boulton Paul aircraft factory.

Pendeford is an ancient settlement. The Barnhurst estate, home of the Cresswell family, was bought by Wolverhampton Council in the 1860s and a sewage works was established there. In 1938 Wolverhampton Airport was opened. It was used as an airfield during the war and finally closed in 1970. A large housing estate and business park now occupies the site.

Certain parts of this area have been frequently photographed while others have been less well served. This collection aims to redress the balance by encompassing the whole region and depicting changes both in landscape and everyday life from the late nineteenth to the middle of the twentieth century. It has been put together by drawing on the collections of many individuals as well as those of Wolverhampton Public Libraries and Codsall Civic Society. Most of the photographs have not been published previously. They have been arranged place by place to give people an insight into the history of their own locality as well as that of the larger area.

Tettenhall and Tettenhall Wood

A VIEW OF TETTENHALL FROM NEWBRIDGE, showing Lower Street and St Michael's church, taken around 1910, before the railway was built alongside Smestow brook and the canal.

NEWBRIDGE BEFORE THE FIRST WORLD WAR showing Weavers Coal Wharf and crowds of people in their Sunday best. Pleasure cruises were available on the canal below the bridge in those days, as they are now, and were a popular pastime.

THE JUNCTION OF HENWOOD ROAD AND TETTENHALL ROAD in 1921. The photograph has been marked to show the Wolverhampton/Tettenhall boundary. A large garage occupies this corner today, although some of the houses still remain.

TETTENHALL RAILWAY STATION from Newbridge. It was opened in 1925 on the Wolverhampton to Kingswinford line. A passenger service operated until 1932 but from then on the station was used only by goods trains, except briefly during the Second World War. It closed completely in 1965. The Valley Park Leisure Walk now follows the route and the station buildings have been refurbished as an information centre.

TETTENHALL ROCK IN THE EARLY TWENTIETH CENTURY. The building on the left was Foxall's, a builder and contractor. On the right is the lodge to Avenue House. The London to Holyhead road originally went up Old Hill and the new road up the Rock was part of the improvement to this route carried out by Thomas Telford in the early 1820s.

CHURCH ROAD LOOKING TOWARDS TETTENHALL ROCK. The cottages and fine old tree on the right have now gone.

LOWER GREEN in the 1890s, a scene which is still much the same. The green is ancient and was originally bigger than today. Local fairs and bull baiting took place on it. The Mitre Inn also has a long history and meetings of the court baron were held there. The advert under Mitre Mews reads 'Broughams, Landaus, Waggonettes etc. for Hire. Special Terms to Wedding and Picnic Parties. Teas etc. Provided. Accommodation for cyclists. A.R. Rowley proprietor'.

TWO VIEWS OF LOWER STREET. The top photograph shows a row of cottages which have now all gone, with the exception of the two next to St Michael's School on the extreme right. St Michael's School first opened in Lower Street as a National School in 1827. The building shown dates from 1888 and it still in use. The photograph below also shows the Swan Inn on the left.

CHURCH WALK, an interesting picture showing the butchers shop at the bottom of the Walk. The shop has been demolished although otherwise the houses remain much the same.

CRESSWELL'S ALMSHOUSES which stood in front of where the present Lower Green Health Centre is. Richard Cresswell made provision in his will for almshouses to be used by six families who had been servants in his household.

THE OLD FIELDHOUSE INN can be seen at the end of this view of Codsall Road. The Claregate public house stands on this site today. The houses on the right remain, but much building has taken place since this photograph was taken.

THE OLD SMITHY AND FORGE COTTAGES which stood on the corner of Clifton Road and Stockwell Road in the late nineteenth century. They were demolished before 1919.

FOR
EVERY
HOUR
THAT
COMES
THERE
IS A
HOPE

I LABOUR
HERE
WITH
ALL MY
MIGHT
TO TELL
THE
HOURS
BY DAY
AND
NIGHT

S 12132 THE CLOCK TOWER, TETTENHALL.

THE CLOCK TOWER was erected in 1911. It was presented by Mr and Mrs Edward Swindley of The Cedars to commemorate the coronation of King George V.

CROWDS AT THE PRESENTATION OF THE CLOCK TOWER on 22 June 1911.

DANESCOURT ROAD, an undated photograph, although the vehicles suggest it may be the '20s or '30s. The row of houses remain unchanged today.

UPPER GREEN LOOKING TOWARDS LIMES ROAD in 1913. The shop in the foreground was Underwood's drapery store and now houses a Building Society. The small cottages next door have been demolished and replaced by a single-storey building now occupied by a greengrocer. The tall building, now a dry cleaners, was a dairy and café run by J. Evans in 1914.

UPPER GREEN, an undated photograph, probably from the first decade of the century. All the buildings remain, except for the single-storey one, and are occupied by a variety of shops. The building on the right, now a delicatessen, belonged to S. Allen, a builder, in 1900.

TWO VIEWS OF UPPER GREEN which appear to have been taken in the 1950s. The photograph above is taken looking into Limes Road with the post office very much as it is today. The picture below looks into the High Street and shows a row of shops and houses on the left that have now been almost entirely replaced by a modern block of shops. The antique shop in the foreground is now a gift shop.

OLD HILL WITH THE ROCK HOTEL in the foreground. The sign reads, 'To the Rock Hotel and Grounds, Bowling Green and Billiards, Arthur Lansdale Proprietor'. The grounds and bowling green were laid out by George Spink in 1843 when he was landlord of the Old Rose and Crown public house, as it was then known. Rock Villa Gardens attracted tourists from Wolverhampton in the 1850s with amusements such as fireworks and balloon ascents.

OLD HILL FROM THE TETTENHALL ROAD. Although this photograph clearly dates from early this century all the buildings still stand and the scene is easily recognizable.

UPPER STREET LOOKING FROM THE TOP OF OLD HILL. The post office is on the right. The postmistress in 1900 was Emma Creighton and letters were delivered three times a day during the week, once on Sundays. The new Rose and Crown can be seen on the left. The publican's name is Postance which dates it around 1900 using Kelly's trade directory. This scene is very different today with only the last few buildings on the right of the street still standing. The rest were demolished in the 1950s to make way for flats.

WOOD ROAD LOOKING TOWARDS TETTENHALL VILLAGE. This view dating from the 1900s appeared on a postcard both in black and white and colour. The house on the left was the lodge to Tettenhall Wood House and still stands, although it is no longer thatched. The road looks little different today, although small housing developments have grown up behind the walls.

WOOD ROAD LOOKING TOWARDS TETTENHALL WOOD. This is another postcard scene with the gates of Tettenhall college on the left.

TROLLEYBUSES AT TETTENHALL TERMINUS. Trolleybuses started to run on the Tettenhall route on 1 January 1928 and it became route No. 1. The adult single fare was 3d. Trolleybuses were frequently photographed in Tettenhall; the photograph below was taken by Wolverhampton's official photographer Bennett Clark for the Town Guide. The shelter was known locally as the Swiss Cottage and started life as a display at the Wolverhampton Art and Industrial Exhibition held in West Park in 1902. It was moved to Wergs road originally as a tram shelter. The last trolleybus ran to Tettenhall on 30 June 1963 and the shelter was demolished in the early 1970s.

AN AERIAL PHOTOGRAPH OF TETTENHALL with St Michael's School in the bottom right-hand corner. Although a fairly recent view, changes can

be seen. The two reservoirs at the top of the picture have now been filled in and houses have been built on the site.

THE CHURCH OF ST MICHAEL AND ALL ANGELS. Many photographs exist of the old church. This one dates from around 1910 and was issued as a postcard.

THE INTERIOR OF ST MICHAEL'S, a very early photograph.

ST MICHAEL'S CHURCH FROM THE TOP OF THE CHURCH WALK. An impressive view showing how large the old church was.

THE RUINS OF ST MICHAEL'S CHURCH after the terrible fire in February 1950. The photograph shows the Bishop of Lichfield, Dr E.S. Woods (facing the camera) with the Vicar of Tettenhall, the Revd C.W. Borrett; Mr R.P. Jenks, vicar's warden, and the Revd R. Lord, curate, surveying the damage.

VOLUNTEERS HELP TO CLEAR THE DEBRIS left after the fire. Only the tower and porch remained after the blaze. There were several reasons why the fire did so much damage; one problem was that the fire-engine was unable to get through the lich-gate, which bears the traces of its attempts to do so to this day. Services were held every week until the new church was complete, firstly among the ruins and later in the restored tower.

THE PRESENT ST MICHAEL'S was consecrated on 16 April 1955. It was designed by Mr Bernard Miller to blend with the restored tower and porch but meet the needs of a modern congregation.

THE FUNERAL OF LIEUTENANT COLONEL THOMAS THORNEYCROFT, known locally as 'Colonel Tom', at St Michael's church in February 1903. The Thorneycroft family were benefactors of St Michael's, presenting ground in front of the church. Many of them are buried in the churchyard.

TETTENHALL TOWERS was the home of Col. Thorneycroft and was very ornately decorated, as can be seen in this picture of the chimney-piece in the theatre. The theatre was complete with a waterfall and stream, and plate glass windows at the back of the stage enabled the audience to see right into the pleasure grounds. The house is now part of Tettenhall College.

LIEUTENANT COLONEL THOMAS THORNEYCROFT (centre) with his band on the occasion of his seventieth birthday. He was a larger than life character who loved organizing and ran a driving club. He was also an inventor who filled Tettenhall Towers with gadgets including signalling equipment at the top of the tower. He involved himself with the local community and even ran his own fire brigade.

WROTTESLEY HALL built in the 1690s. Before that time there was a village and hall but most of the cottages were demolished by a Roundhead garrison which occupied the hall during the Civil War. The Wolverhampton — Shrewsbury road passed close to the hall but was rerouted in the early 1800s to follow the Newport road as far as Kingswood.

THE RUINS OF WROTTESLEY HALL. The hall was destroyed by fire in 1897 and stood in ruins for many years. Photographs in Wolverhampton Library collection suggest that the ruins were something of a tourist attraction.

WROTTESLEY HALL AFTER IT WAS REBUILT in 1923 by the fourth Lord Wrottesley. The new building was designed by F.T. Beck and based on the foundation of the previous one, re-using some of the original materials. It is very similar to the original building, although on a smaller scale. The house is, at present, divided up into three separate homes.

WERGS HALL. The hall dates from around 1860 and was built by the Fryer family to replace a previous house. It was bought by McAlpine's in 1963 to be used as offices.

THE CONSERVATORY AT WERGS HALL. Both this photograph and the one above show how spectacular the gardens and plants were when the hall was still a private residence.

DANES COURT PHOTOGRAPHED SHORTLY BEFORE IT WAS DEMOLISHED in 1958. The house was built in 1860 by Edward Perry, a Wolverhampton tin smith and japanner. His firm was the forerunner of the Sunbeam Motor Company. In 1908 the house was bought by Edward Hickman the industrialist; when he died in 1941 it was occupied by troops and then by the Territorial Army.

WOODTHORNE was built near to Danes Court in 1867 for H.H. Fowler who later became Viscount Wolverhampton. The house was used by the Ministry of Agriculture and Fisheries from 1946 until 1978 when it was demolished to make way for new offices for the Ministry.

TETTENHALL CHURCH PARADE, 1904

FILLING SANDBAGS to protect the council offices in 1939. Tettenhall was a separate Urban District until most of the area became part of Wolverhampton borough in 1966. The council offices were formerly a private house called Oaklands and now house Tettenhall Regis library.

ST MICHAEL'S SCHOOL in 1920. The boy in the sailor suit on the second row from the back, third from the left, is Charles Woodhouse.

FISHER GIRLS, ST MICHAEL'S SCHOOL in 1915. Back row, left to right: Winnie Arkinstall, Ethel Dimmock, Olive Morris, Jean Barratt. Front row: Dorothy Kendrick, Elsie Cox.

ST MICHAEL'S GIRLS' SCHOOL. Edith Humphries is on the far right of the second row.

ST MICHAEL'S BOYS' SCHOOL. The Eton suits worn by these boys date this to before the First World War. Only the relatively well-off would have been able to afford them. An advertisement for Buxton and Bonnetts in the 1905 Webb's Annual gives the price as twenty-one shillings.

THE DOG AND GUN WROTTESLEY ROAD. While the pub still stands, the cottages next door have made way for a car park. The photograph is not dated, but the Dog and Gun has a long history. It is described in an article dated 1891 as being recently modernized and a list of six previous landlords is given.

THE BOWLING GREEN AT THE ROCK HOTEL. The man standing fourth from the left is James Dalton. The Daltons are a long-established Tettenhall Wood family who were prominent in the building trade.

UNDERWOOD, THE DRAPERS SHOP on the corner of High Street and Upper Green, in 1911. The decorations to celebrate George V's coronation can be seen above the name. George Underwood stands in the doorway. His son, wearing the grammar school cap, was killed in the First World War. The shop sold drapery, ladies shoes and also carpets. Before 1910 he had another shop, believed to have been in Bilston.

EDWARD HICKMAN'S CHAUFFEUR, WALTER HUMPHRIES, and other servants outside Danes Court. The girl second from the left was Edith Lowe. Danes Court cottages, which still stand on the bend of Danescourt Road, were built to house Hickman's chauffeur and butler. The car behind was used to drive Mr Hickman to his steelworks at Bilston each day.

FAYE JONES IN SERVICE IN TETTENHALL. She is pictured in the middle of the group and worked for two doctors called O'Dowd in Stockwell End from 1919 when she was fourteen years old. The photograph was taken when her employers gave a party, the other two maids having been brought in for the occasion.

TWO VIEWS OF WOOD ROAD. Above, the Lodge to Tettenhall Wood is shown but now with a slate roof. Below, some cottages which still stand today. The cottage with the lady outside has a sign which reads 'Homelight Lamp Oil'.

LOOKING FROM WOOD ROAD INTO MOUNT ROAD. This photograph dates from before 1956 and shows the old shop on the corner of School Road. Tettenhall Wood Institute is in the foreground.

SCHOOL ROAD. A postcard view which would appear to date from around the 1940s. The Royal Oak can be seen on the left; the house adjoining it has gone. The row of cottages beyond the telephone kiosk have been demolished and shops built in their place. The former Christ Church School was built as a National School in 1874. The school moved to a new building in 1976.

THE JUNCTION OF THE HOLLOWAY, ORMES LANE AND CHURCH ROAD. This postcard view remains much the same except that the gateway on the left has been blocked up and houses built behind the wall.

THESE COTTAGES AT LONG LAKE show clearly the very poor conditions that existed in the areas that were rarely photographed away from the postcard views. The cottages lay behind School Road along a dirt track where Long Lake Avenue runs today. The family are believed to be the Dalloways. The area was known as Brickkiln and the houses were not demolished until the 1940s.

TETTENHALL WOOD INSTITUTE was opened as a workmen's reading room in 1887 and moved into this building in 1893. In 1896 anyone over eighteen who lived in Tettenhall Wood, Compton and environs could become a member. The subscription was 1s. 6d. a quarter from October to April and 6d. a quarter for the rest of the year. The facilities available were a reading room, smoke room and bagatelle room.

TETTENHALL WORKHOUSE, Brych House, which was situated in Wrottesley Road just west of the junction with Redhouse Road and was bought for the poor in 1714. By 1746 it had become a workhouse. After several extensions it ceased to be used for this purpose in 1860.

TETTENHALL WOOD CONGREGATIONAL CHURCH. This photograph is taken from Webb's Annual of 1905, when it was a branch of Queen Street Congregational church. The minister at the time was the Revd Henry Gardner. The building was opened in 1873, largely through the efforts of S.S. Mander.

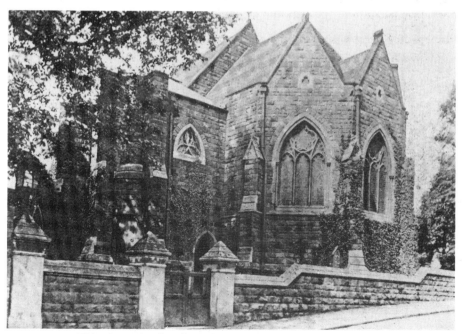

CHRIST CHURCH. This picture is taken from the same source as above. The church opened in 1866 and was paid for largely by voluntary contributions.

THE GROVE before the Second World War, home of H.T. Fullwood.

THE GROVE AFTER BEING HIT BY A BOMB during the war. One night a German plane jettisoned three bombs. One flattened the Grove, one damaged Elmhurst and the third fell in woodland on the opposite side of the road. The force was sufficient to blow a lady in Ormes Lane clean out of bed.

THE GROVE AFTER REBUILDING. It was, in turn, demolished and a residential development has taken its place.

TETTENHALL WOOD HOUSE. This house stood near the end of the present Grange Road and the drive came out on Wood Road where the lodge still stands. It belonged to the Hickman family and was demolished around 1970.

AFCOT, another of the large Tettenhall Wood houses. It stood behind Christ Church and was built between 1889 and 1919. The site is now occupied by a block of flats but the coach-house still stands in Grove Lane.

THE MOUNT was built around 1865 by C.B. Mander on the site of an earlier house. The Mander family had a paint and varnish business in Wolverhampton and a long association with the town. Extensions were added to the house at various times. The house was sold and converted into a hotel in 1951 after the death of Sir Geoffrey Mander.

VALE HEAD DURING A GARDEN PARTY in the 1950s. The house stood on the corner of Mount Road and Wightwick Bank and was demolished and replaced by a block of flats called Wightwick Court. The Bruford family lived there in the 1930s.

CHRIST CHURCH SCHOOL in 1921. The two teachers are (left) Miss Winnie Dace and (right) Mrs J. Perry. From left to right, top row: Bill Taft, George Crane, Bill Pearce, Harold Bowker, Lily Davies, Nancy Cotteril, Edith Whale, Alexea Jones, Dorothy Walker. Second row: Tim Bond, Meggy Peel, Gwen Jones, Milly Handie, Hilda Dalton, Marg Postance, ? Dalton, Bill Thorneycroft, Kitty Bennett. Third row: Harry Carter, Alice Baxter, Edna York, Gladys Alport, Marg Dunn, Marie Jones, Maggie Gabb, Gladys Burns, Harry Evans, George Clayton. Front row: Walter Tooth, Wilf Dalloway, Herbert Tooth, Redge Clements, Reg Hollinghead, Charlee Burden, Alfred Till, George Law.

CHRIST CHURCH INFANTS SCHOOL FIRST CLASS. The infants school was built in 1844 and was rebuilt in Shaw Lane in 1963. The original building is now Tettenhall Wood Library.

CHRIST CHURCH FOOTBALL TEAM 1934/35. From left to right, back: Harold Pye, Bert Norgrove, ? Tranter. Middle: Harold Yates, Bert Walters, Pete Lloyd, Roy Meek, John Weston. Front: Harry Jones, Bill Guy, Horace Howell, Maurice Wheeler.

CHRIST CHURCH INFANTS in 1922. Back row; first and second left, Mary and Peggy Pritchard; fourth and fifth right, ? Fisher, J. Holt; far right, G. Woodhouse. Second row; third left, ? Pye; fourth right, ? Taylor. Third row; fourth left, ? Cain; fourth and fifth right, the Lowe sisters; second right, ? Humpherson. Front row; first left, ? Ponstance; second left, P. Howel; fourth left, ? Roberts; third right, ? Salter; far right, ? Humpherson.

TETTENHALL WOOD BOY SCOUTS 1936/7. Among the group are Eric Curral, Bill Guy, Harold Pye, Bert Richards, Maurice Wheeler, Dennis Hume, Harry Preston, Arthur Taylor, Horace Howell, Maurice Wheeler.

SCOUTS M. Wheeler, H. Yates and H. Pye in 1938

MISS LOCKLEY'S SHOP on the corner of Mount Road and School Road. There is a florists shop on this site now. Miss Lockley is pictured outside. She sold groceries and homemade bread.

INSIDE MISS LOCKLEY'S SHOP in 1942. The photograph shows Gertrude Lockley, Sylvia Lockley and Sally Taylor. This interior view is unusual and there are some interesting advertisements on the shelves for products that are no longer in use, such as 'RINSO washes while you sleep'.

THE ROYAL OAK BOWLS TEAM. It is interesting to see that no women feature in this photograph but boys and animals were included.

THE SHOULDER OF MUTTON, Wood Road, which was demolished in 1980 to make way for a new pub of the same name. The building is believed to be over 150 years old and to have been used originally as a butchers shop. The first record in a trade directory is for 1876 when the landlady was Sarah Jeavons.

THE CHURCH

THE WOODS

CORONATION MEMORIAL TOWER

TETTENHALL.
Nr. WOLVERHAMPTON.

THE CANAL

LOWER GREEN

A POSTCARD SHOWING VARIOUS ASPECTS OF TETTENHALL. The view of 'The Woods' shows the most change.

Compton and Wightwick

COMPTON ROAD, LOOKING INTO THE VILLAGE in the days before the motor car. The row of buildings on the right in the background have been demolished and a block of shops now stands on the site. The cottages in the foreground still stand and are at present being renovated.

THE BOAT INN. The date it was built is not clear but it was later than the canal which came in 1766. In 1851 it appears in White's directory and the landlord was Walter Phillips. The building originally stood some feet above the level of the road until the road was improved. The building existed as a private house until the 1950s. Compton Farm can be seen in the background next to Lodge Farm, the small cottage which is still there today.

COMPTON RAILWAY BRIDGE. The railway was built in 1925 and the photograph would appear to date from the 1930s from the car and the advertisements on the bridge. The old Oddfellows can be seen in the background.

COMPTON COAL WHARF on the canalside was kept by L.T. Law from 1896. The lady in the cart is his wife. Compton Hall can just be seen.

COMPTON HALL in the days when it was a private house, with the gardeners attending to the lawn. It was built in the mid-nineteenth century and bought by Thomas Elwell, a Wolverhampton hardware merchant, in 1828. It later passed into the Hodson family who had interests in the Springfield Brewery. The house contained some notable furnishings: William Morris wallpaper and Burne-Jones tapestries. After the Second World War it became a nurses' home and in 1982 Compton Hospice.

COTTAGES AND SHOPS on the corner where the Wolverhampton – Bridgnorth Road bends sharply. All have now gone. The cottages are on the site now occupied by the new Oddfellows public house and restaurant.

COMPTON VILLAGE in the 1950s. On the left is Bown's bakery where the modern freezer centre stands. The cottages shown in the photograph above have now gone but the shops are still there. The first after the Oddfellows was a paper shop; next, Williams, the greengrocer; then

GLADYS WATKINS, Compton postlady in the fifties when the mail was sorted in the green wooden hut just under the railway bridge and the post office stood at the end of the row of cottages opposite.

Mountfords sweet shop and Coopers, the butcher. The single-storey building was a fish shop. The other buildings were houses and were demolished in the 1960s. A modern block of shops behind a lay-by have replaced them. The Swan on the right is still there.

THE MILL POOL, HENWOOD ROAD. The mill stood at the Compton end of the road from the seventeenth century, and the first pool was where the boys' club and playing field are today. This view is Edwardian and shows how rural this area was then. By 1919 the mill was disused and the two pools had been drained.

HENWOOD ROAD in the 1920s. This view is from further up the road near to where the prefabs are today. The Elms can be seen in the background.

THE NEWBRIDGE END OF HENWOOD ROAD before the railway was built. The houses at the corner of Tettenhall Road can be seen to the left.

THE STAFFORDSHIRE AND WORCESTERSHIRE CANAL, looking towards Newbridge. This stretch of canal has long been used for leisure and has consequently been much photographed.

THE CANAL, LOOKING FROM COMPTON BRIDGE towards Compton Lock. The cottage on the left has gone although part of the wall is still there. The lock is reputed to be the first ever built by James Brindley, and the pattern for all subsequent ones.

AN EDWARDIAN FAMILY posed in front of the cottage that stood at Compton Lock.

THE COTTAGE AT COMPTON LOCK. The Beech family lived here and ran a pleasure boat business in the 1920s. One of the rowing boats can be seen on the canal. A path led from here to Compton Farm.

MRS BEECH AND HER DAUGHTER at Warren Truss Bridge in 1926.

ARTHUR BEECH WITH HIS WIFE AND SON. The pleasure steamer *Compton Queen* can be seen behind. Mr Beech ran three such steamers, the other two named *Margaret* and *Victoria*, from Newbridge. They made afternoon cruises to Coven, Calf Heath or Brewood. Adults paid 1s. and children 6d.

THE DALTON FAMILY FROM TETTENHALL WOOD waiting for a boat trip at Newbridge. From right to left: Roland Tattershall, Sarah Dalton (first Tettenhall midwife), Staveley Dalton, Granny Howe, Nellie Dalton (the baby), Lucy (the young girl), Dot, John and other cousins. The date was around 1900.

ALFRED WHEELER OUTSIDE COMPTON FARM. The farm was in the Wheeler family for many years. Walter Wheeler, his father, originally rented it from Clara Elwell, widow of Revd W.F. Elwell, from 1883 and it was sold by Alfred in 1925.

HAYMAKING AT COMPTON FARM. The land ran down to the canal. The cover photograph shows a threshing machine at the farm around 1920. Alfred Wheeler stands on the right of both photographs.

BUILDING OF THE WARREN TRUSS BRIDGE which carried the railway over the canal. It is known locally as the 'Meccano' bridge and is now a feature on the Valley Park Linear Walk.

CUTTING THE RAILWAY AT COMPTON. The workmen's tents can be seen at the top of the hill.

WORKMEN ENGAGED ON BUILDING THE RAILWAY through Compton. This photograph and the one opposite (below) were both taken on land belonging to Compton Farm. Walter Wheeler sold the land to the Great Western Railway Company in 1905 although the line was not completed until 1925.

COMPTON HALT. While Tettenhall had a station, Compton was just a halt with a small shelter. This photograph was taken in August 1926 at the start of a trip to the Orton Hills, Wombourne. It shows from left to right: Pat Johnson (half hidden), Sylvia Cox, Mrs Cox (hidden behind Sylvia) Dennis Johnson, Miss Marjorie Adams, Cecil Cox, Phyllis Cox (behind him), Keith Johnson.

ROYAL PIERROTS AT COMPTON in 1905. This troop claimed to be 'Original', 'Refined' and 'Up-to-date' and to have appeared in front of royalty. The manager Mr Hamilton Baines paid Joseph Walker, a local coal merchant, two pounds to rent his field for a month and arranged with the Chief Constable to have a police officer present each evening.

COMPTON FLOWER SHOW, 1916. The flower show dated back to 1878 and in the 1880s was held either at the Boat Inn or in the grounds of Compton Hall. As well as the flower displays and competitions, sports were held and entertainments arranged. The photograph suggests that there was also a fancy dress competition by 1916, and would appear to have been taken at Compton Farm. There are two mounted special constables. The one on the left is Alfred Wheeler.

THE ODDFELLOWS HALL at the turn of the century. The landlord, Hope Till, is listed in trade directories as a beer retailer. This building stood at the rear of the site of the present Oddfellows, behind the cottages shown on page 60, and was demolished around 1937. Local residents still remember the monkey puzzle tree.

THE BOAT INN. This view looking towards Wolverhampton shows the cottages that were also in the row. The kerbstones and railings in front have only recently been removed. Houses have been built in Captains Close, behind the site, and the land has been brought back up to the level of the road.

THE SWAN INN. This is one of the oldest pubs in the area, dating back at least to 1780, and was originally a coaching inn. The cottages alongside were demolished in the 1960s and a car park has taken their place.

COMPTON HOLLOWAY looking down towards The Swan around 1910. The railings at the side remain, but modern houses have been built further down. The view towards Finchfield was very rural then, but the area has been steadily built up, especially since the late 1940s.

WIGHTWICK BANK showing how steep the side of this ridge is. Again a scene that is little changed, although the road has been widened.

VIEWLANDS which stands at the top of Wightwick Bank with a lodge on the Bridgnorth Road was originally called Elmsdale Hall and was built in the 1860s. In 1914 it was bought by Jesse Varley, clerk to the Education Authority, with some of the £84,335 4s. 7d. he embezzled from Wolverhampton Council between 1905 and 1917, when he was discovered, arrested and sentenced to five years penal servitude. It was occupied by a Miss Swift in 1919 and she changed the name. Recently it has been an elderly persons' home but it is currently being converted to flats and is to be known as Elmsdale again. Jesse Varley later repeated his crime in another local authority.

VISIT OF THE DUKE AND DUCHESS OF YORK (later George V and Queen Mary) to Wightwick Manor, 23 July 1900 when Theodore Mander was Mayor of Wolverhampton. Wightwick Manor was built by Theodore Mander in 1887. He planned to build a model housing development along the Bridgnorth Road and to further extend the Manor but, although some houses were built in 1893 in a style similar to the Manor, the scheme was never completed. The house was designed by Edward Ould, a specialist in half-timbered buildings, and was decorated inside by William Morris. It was given to the National Trust in 1937 although Lady Rosalie Mander continued to live in it until her death in 1988 and the family retain private apartments.

THE MANDER FAMILY AT WIGHTWICK on the occasion of Lady Mander's ninetieth birthday, 12 March 1948. Mary, Lady Mander is seated in the middle. On her right are Sir Charles Mander, Mrs Patrick Stirling, Mrs James Ramsden, Marcus Mander. On her left are Gerald Mander, Daphne Mander, Philip Mander and Mrs William Purslow. Behind Charles stands, from left to right: Sir Geoffrey Mander, Miss Daisy St Clair Mander, Mrs Jarvis Nevile and Peter Nevile.

THE STAFFORDSHIRE AND WORCESTERSHIRE CANAL at Wightwick with Wightwick Manor in the background.

THE MERMAID INN taken about 1896 when Sarah Hawkins was landlord, before the canopy was put up at the front and the Bridgnorth Road was widened.

THE MERMAID INN showing the smithy that stood in front. Theodore Mander bought the inn around 1900 and rented part of it to the Poeple's Refreshment House Association, a temperance organization. Although alcohol continued to be served in part of the building, teas, minerals, etc. were also available. This arrangement persisted into the 1950s. The inn was a favourite tourist halt and had a bowling green where the upper part of the car park now stands. By the door on the left is a sign 'To the Tea Room'.

WIGHTWICK HALL WITH ITS FORMER OWNER SIR ALFRED HICKMAN who owned the steelworks at Bilston. The hall was originally built in the seventeenth century but was bought by Theodore Mander in 1887 and rebuilt by Ould, the designer of Wightwick Manor. The Hickman family lived there from the 1890s until 1932. The hall is now a special school.

WIGHTWICK FROM WINDMILL BANK. The line of the Bridgnorth Road can be seen with the Mermaid and houses built by Theodore Mander.

ALF. WALKER WIGHTWICK WHARF.

WIGHTWICK WHARF in 1928 when it was owned by Alfred Walker. He was a coal merchant and son of Joseph Walker who had a coal wharf at Compton. He bought the land from the Manders and had the house built. The small building shown was a weighbridge. The wharf now houses a boatyard.

THE YARD AT WIGHTWICK WHARF. Sand was quarried from pits on Windmill Bank, near where the nature reserve is now. Until the 1930s the sand was moved in trucks that were tipped directly into barges waiting below.

THE WIGHTWICK FIELDHOUSE, PERTON ROAD. Alfred Walker kept the pub before he started his business at Wightwick Wharf. He is on the photograph in the foreground, next to the man with the horse. He previously kept the Ball at Coven. The inn probably dates back to 1780.

SECTION THREE

Perton and Pendeford

A DEFIANT, manufactured by Boulton Paul Aircraft Ltd shortly before the last war, photographed at Pendeford.

AN AERIAL VIEW OF PERTON taken in 1963 showing the airfield. The road passing the airfield on the right is Wrottesley Park Road which reaches a crossroads where it meets Jenny Walker's Lane, Perton Road and Pattingham Road. The houses along Perton Ridge can be seen to the right, as can Tinacre Hill on the left. There was an airstrip at Perton during the First World War and the site was considered for a borough airport in the 1930s. However, the airfield did not open until 28 August 1941. It was used as a training ground throughout the war and also for testing and repairing planes. The RAF abandoned Perton in 1947 and a large housing estate has been built on the site.

DUTCH TROOPS from the Princess Wilhelmina and Princess Irene brigades were stationed at Perton during the war. A camp was established at Wrottesley Park, between the airfield and the Wergs Road. These two photographs show the camp under construction.

A GENERAL VIEW OF THE CAMP AT WROTTESLEY showing the huts.

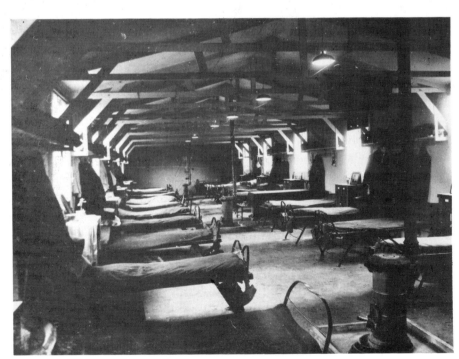

INSIDE ONE OF THE HUTS AT THE CAMP.

QUEEN WILHELMINA VISITS THE TROOPS. The Dutch brigades were formed from Netherlands military personnel who had escaped from the Netherlands, from Dutchmen who had been recruited in England, America, Canada and South Africa, and also from volunteers. The Princess Irene Brigade later fought in France and took part in the liberation of the Low Countries.

PERTON in the 1950s taken from a track leading off Yew Tree Lane. After the RAF left, the land went back to agriculture and the buildings were occupied by squatters. The old runways were used by motor cyclists and learner drivers. Sir Charles Mander who owned most of the land applied for permission to build in 1963, and despite initial opposition the scheme went ahead and building started in 1974.

ALFRED WHEELER cutting a path from Perton Road into Boundary Farm during the severe winter of 1947.

PERTON GROVE which stood behind Perton Road opposite Boundary Farm. The photograph dates from the 1940s and shows Mr and Mrs Wheeler who lived in the lodge near to Boundary Farm. They are on the right of the group and their son Maurice is on the left.

PENDEFORD AIRPORT in 1948. The site was purchased in 1935 and the airport was opened in 1938. It was operated by The Midland Aero Club until it was requisitioned by the RAF when war broke out and became a training station. In 1953 Don Everall Aviation applied to operate scheduled flights to the Isle of Man and Wolverhampton Aviation ran flights to Jersey. Wolverhampton Aero club also ran a private club and flying displays were held in the 1950s.

THE INTERIOR OF BOULTON PAUL AIRCRAFT FACTORY during the Second World War. The firm moved to a site next to the projected airfield in 1936, the parent company being in Ipswich. They used the runways on the airfield for testing their planes. The plane shown under construction was the Blackburn Roc and the date around 1940.

A PROTOTYPE OF THE BOULTON PAUL DEFIANT at Pendeford. The Defiant played an important role in aircraft development being the first fighter fitted with a rear-facing gun turret. The company built 1,060 of these planes.

SIR STAFFORD CRIPPS (far right of group) visits Boulton Paul during the war. Women were drafted in to boost the workforce numbers.

APPRENTICES AT BOULTON PAUL'S around 1950. Front row, far right, Alan Hughes. From left to right, second row: Roy Conway, George Rous, Ray Anthony, Lewis Chesney, -?-, Horace Jones, ? Reynolds, ? Ford, Tom Flavell, Ken Slaney, Brian Tovell, Pete Taylor. Third row: Alan Butler, Clive Birchall, Dave Young, ? Fellows, -?-, Tony Southwood, -?-, Goodman, -?-. Back row, from left to right: Haycocks; fifth, Alan Green; tenth, John Taff; Brian Castley; George Richards; fourth from right, Pete Stone; Reg Green; Archie Onions; last, Phil Harris.

PENDEFORD AIRPORT showing the control tower. During the '60s it was a busy airfield but, nevertheless, it was decided that it was not necessary for Wolverhampton to have its own airport and the idea of using the site for a housing estate was put forward. There was much opposition but an accident in 1970, when the occupant of a house nearby was killed, sealed its fate. A large housing estate has been built and a new business park is soon to open.

A SCHOOL VISIT by pupils of Princes End, 10 June 1956.

THE FILM *MAN IN THE SKY* was made at Pendeford in 1956. It starred Jack Hawkins, who was asked to open Aldersley Stadium during his time here. The airport also featured on *Crossroads*, the soap opera, during the '60s.

PENDEFORD FARM. This may have been the house for Upper Farm which has now been demolished or possibly Pendeford Mill which stood opposite the gate of Boulton Paul's.

THE LLOYD/JAMES FAMILY of Pendeford Farm.

LEO JAMES, BARNHURST FARM. It would appear that Leo James was connected with the Lloyd/James family of Pendeford Farm. Barnhurst Farm was also worked as a farm until 1975, although the estate has been owned by Wolverhampton Council since 1867 and used primarily for the disposal of sewage. Possibly the two farms were worked together.

THE GATEHOUSE OF THE ORIGINAL BARNHURST FARM which was demolished in 1963. The dovecote which can be seen has been preserved and has given the name 'Dovecotes' to part of the Pendeford estate. The Barnhurst Estate dated back to the thirteenth century.

PENDEFORD HALL stood behind the site of the present mobile home park on Pendeford Hall Lane. It was built some time before 1780 and demolished in 1953.

SECTION FOUR

Codsall and Bilbrook

THE COTTAGE AT DAM MILL on the junction of Codsall Road, Birches Road and Lane Green Road before 1910. The couple pictured are William and Ellen Smith. He was a gardener at the Birches.

AN AERIAL VIEW taken in 1955 before the bypass was built in the early 1970s. Baker's nurseries can be seen in the foreground with Church Road running diagonally from the left and continuing as Station Road. There is a train standing at the station (top right).

A GENERAL VIEW taken before the modern housing estates were built in the '60s showing the prominent position of St Nicholas's church. The old vicarage can be seen to the left of the church.

A VIEW TAKEN FROM THE TOP OF THE CHURCH TOWER again showing how rural Codsall was until recent times. The photograph is looking down Church Road and dates from the early part of the century.

ST NICHOLAS'S CHURCH viewed from an unusual angle. There has been a church on this site since the twelfth century and in the early days Codsall looked to Tettenhall as its mother church. The present building, with the exception of the Norman tower, dates from 1849 and was restored in 1958.

THE CHESTNUT TREE outside the church gate which is probably the site of a village green. Judging by the cars this view dates from the 1920s. It was sold as a postcard.

CHURCH ROAD LOOKING TOWARDS THE CHURCH. The photograph probably dates from the turn of the century, showing cobbles that do not appear on later views. The house and the wall to Manor Court on the left remain, but all the cottages on the right have been demolished and replaced by modern housing.

CHURCH ROAD with Russell House, formerly Bakers Buildings, in the foreground. The bypass now runs where the two girls are standing and the doctors use the house for their surgery. The photograph dates from before the First World War and was taken by Bennett Clark. The house behind the two smaller girls is where Sir Charles Wheeler, the sculptor, was born.

CHURCH ROAD in 1961. The cottages on the left are still lived in. Those on the right, which were some of the oldest buildings in Codsall, have since been demolished.

THE OLDEST BUILDING IN CODSALL, often called the Manor House, dates back to the seventeenth century. It has been used as an antique shop and is now a restaurant. The cottages alongside have now gone.

THE BOTTOM END OF CHURCH ROAD where it opened into the Square showing the post office in the 1930s. The building is still there and now houses a Building Society. The bypass now crosses behind, blocking off this part of Church Road.

THE BULL in 1935, which stood on what was then the main road and was kept by T.H. Athersmith. It was described as having 'good motor accommodation, pleasure grounds and bowling green'. On the other corner is York's Grocery and Provision Stores which continued to be known as York's long after it had changed hands. In 1935 it was run by C.A. Stockton. This was one of a series of postcards of Codsall compiled by W.F. Crane as a souvenir of George V's Silver Jubilee.

THE SQUARE SHOWING THE CROWN.

ANOTHER VIEW OF THE SQUARE with people carefully posed. Judging by the clothes the photograph dates from around 1910. Trade directories list the proprietor of the Crown as Thomas Malpas, also a butcher and farmer, in 1900. Charles Malpas was the proprietor in 1924. It seems possible that the son took over from his father between these two dates. The road to the left of the Crown is Wood Road and was the bus route to Codsall Wood until the bypass was built.

COTTAGES IN WILKES ROAD. The main road into Codsall from Wolverhampton originally followed the line of Wilkes Road until it was re-aligned in the early 1800s. These cottages stood near the junction with Station Road. The man in the doorway is the late Mr Orpett.

THE WAR MEMORIAL ON STATION ROAD.

LOOKING DOWN STATION ROAD from the station bridge around the turn of the century. The road where the carriage is turning is where Fairfield Drive is today.

CHILDREN POSE IN FRONT OF THE STATION. The Shrewsbury – Wolverhampton line opened in 1850. Children used to sledge down this slope in the 1940s and '50s.

AN EDWARDIAN LADY AT THE ENTRANCE TO OAKEN DRIVE, formerly Oaken Avenue, leading to Springfield House and Oaken Terrace.

RIVOLI, SUCKLING GREEN LANE, which was originally two cottages and called Peewit Castle. It is now painted white and stands at right angles to the road.

A POSTCARD VIEW OF ELLIOTS LANE around 1930. The houses on the left are still there but otherwise the road looks very different.

HISTONS HILL in the 1930s with the wall of Woodfield on the right. The 1884 map shows Woodfield as one of only four houses in Histons Hill and a quarry is marked at the junction with Chapel Lane. Even in 1930 there were very few houses in this part of Codsall.

WOOD ROAD showing a row of houses, dating from the late nineteenth and early twentieth century, built to accommodate the tradesmen and clerks who worked in Wolverhampton, Bilston and Wednesbury. The housing of commuters in Codsall dates from the building of the railway.

MOATBROOK LANE looking into Wood Road. The water splash was a favourite haunt of young boys bent on mischief in the 1940s and '50s. People also used to stop and wash their cars in it.

WOOD HALL FROM THE SOUTH showing the remainder of the moat in front of the house. It was bought by the Gaskell family in the later 1920s from the Ward family and the photograph dates from around that time. The building shown dates from around 1835 and replaced a thirteenth-century house which stood surrounded by the moat.

BIRCHES FARM, WOLVERHAMPTON ROAD before 1910. The farm is still there and originally stood next to The Birches. The family are Walter Worskett, coachman from The Birches, with his wife and two daughters, Lena and Ethel.

TRINITY FREE CHURCH AND SCHOOL, Chapel Lane, 1935. It was built in 1873/4. S.S. Mander of Queen Street Congregational church was involved in its foundation. In 1956 it became Trinity Methodist church and in 1967 the congregation moved into a new building on Histons Hill and the old chapel was demolished.

ST CHRISTOPHER'S ROMAN CATHOLIC CHURCH in 1935. The church was built in 1934 by Louis Connolly of Wolverhampton, as a memorial to his wife Henrietta. Prior to this, there had been no church for local Catholics and, for a time, mass was said in a Codsall tea shop. The building was extended in the early 1960s.

BAKER'S NURSERIES with Russell House in Church Road visible in the background, just left of centre. It was one of several nurseries in the area. Baker's was established between 1900 and 1904 and closed in the late 1960s. There was a Baker's seed shop in Queen Square, Wolverhampton and they also produced catalogues to sell by mail order. The nursery was famous for the Russell Lupin and also for its landscaping.

CODSALL SUPPLY COMPANY in 1935. The business started in 1920 as a coal merchants. In 1921 they bought Calf Heath Mill and traded in corn and general agricultural products. By 1935 the firm employed twenty-four people and supplied farms within a fifteen mile radius using their own fleet of vehicles. Their premises stood in Station Road close to where the Co-operative supermarket is now.

CODSALL CYCLE STORES, 1935, when J. Hancock had the agency for Sunbeam, BSA, Hercules, etc. He also sold gramophone records and gun cartridges. This is another of the Jubilee postcards.

BIRCHES BRIDGE GARAGE in 1935, on the same site as today. The proprietor was W. Brindley and the family still run the garage, now under the name of Brincars. In 1935 they were agents for Morris cars and also for Raleigh and Hercules cycles. There used to be a sweet shop on the corner nearby.

THE REPAIR AND SERVICE GARAGE of A. Harper and J. Wall which once stood on Wolverhampton Road, 1935. The two partners had worked for Sunbeam Motors before they started their own business. The petrol pump supplied Shell Mex petrol. The house and garage are still there, near to the police station.

THE SMITHY AND FORGE. W.G. Harvey combined the trades of blacksmith, wheelwright, agricultural repairer, carpenter and undertaker. Already in 1935 he was having to keep abreast of changing times and also provided a battery charging service and a car for hire. He later ran a taxi service.

THE CODSALL MOTOR BUS IN THE SQUARE. The man on the right is Mr Powell.

THE POST OFFICE in 1935, again a Jubilee postcard. In 1935 there were 858 houses in the Codsall postal area, with a population of about 3,500. There were three deliveries and four collections of letters daily. The postmaster was J.L. Law.

ALCOCK'S BUTCHERS SHOP which stood on the site now occupied by a central heating firm in Chapel Lane. The hoarding behind advertising Codsall Supply Company was along the side of the railway.

FRANK SPENCER, BUTCHER, in 1935. All meat was killed and dressed on the premises. Mr Spencer was assisted by his son Harry, who was also a farmer and raised his own cattle.

SCREENS HAIRDRESSERS, which was considered very up to date in 1935. The shop also catered for smokers, selling cigarettes, etc. The business appears to have been founded after 1932.

CODSALL MANUAL TELEPHONE EXCHANGE which was situated in Elmhurst on Wood Road. It opened in 1908 and in 1967 became automatic and moved to Histons Hill. The photograph was taken about 1964. The couple at the back are Mr and Mrs Aston who were the original operators and caretakers of the building.

THE WHEEL INN. The photograph above is from the 1935 series. The landlord, George McLachlan, had been there since 1932 and had recently modernized and extended the premises. The view below is from the 1920s when Thomas Bentley was the publican. In 1896 Thomas Bentley was described as publican and wheelwright, and the smaller building on the right was his workshop. The photograph shows three generations of his family. From left to right: Beatrice and Jane, his daughters; Maud Clark, his niece; Thomas himself; Annie Clark, his sister; Vera Taylor née Rudge (little girl); Alice Rudge, his daughter; Daniel Rudge and Eleanor Rudge (Alice's children).

THE OPENING OF THE NEW CO-OPERATIVE STORES in 1968. Codsall had had a branch of the Wolverhampton Co-operative Society in Church Road since at least 1924. The roof of Codsall House can be seen to the left. On the right is the post office.

FESTIVAL OF BRITAIN PARADE, 21 July 1951. The Festival Queen was Marion Walker.

THE ALBRIGHTON HUNT meet outside the Crown in 1932. The Crown has clearly been modernized since the earlier photographs were taken.

BEATING THE BOUNDS in 1935. This ancient ceremony took place once a year in all parishes, when members of a parish walked its boundaries to ensure they remained intact. The last year this took place in Codsall was 1935. Traditionally sticks were carried to 'beat' out the boundaries. Included in the group are Captain Warner (seventh from left), Mr Duckers (in front with a cigarette and stick), and Mrs Scott (in the middle with a walking stick) who was chairman of the parish council at the time.

ARMISTICE DAY SERVICE, 1932, at the war memorial in Station Road.

ARMISTICE DAY PROCESSION passing the war memorial in 1930.

THE PRESENTATION OF PEACE MUGS in Codsall Square, 1918.

RED CROSS PARADE during the First World War, possibly in Landsdowne Road.

THE COLLAPSE OF A WALL IN CHURCH ROAD, thought to have happened around 1908 when two horses pulling a brewer's dray bolted in Sandy Lane.

GEORGE RUSSELL OF BAKER'S NURSERY pictured in 1938 with a field of his famous strain of
Lupin.

TOM BRIGHT'S FATHER, 'BRIGHT', who was the woodman at Pendrell Hall. His photograph appeared in Baker's Seed catalogues when they needed a 'character' to illustrate one of their products.

PIPPIN AND MAISIE BURD, daughters of Dr Burd, with their cat Whitsen Boss.

DR BURD LIVED AT LANESIDE, Oaken Lanes, and was the village doctor for many years. He made his rounds with a pony and trap, seen here waiting for him with Wilkins the coachman. The horse was called Bessie.

DR AND MRS BURD IN THEIR DE DION CAR outside Laneside. Dr Burd became a doctor as it was his only means of joining the navy, and came to Codsall after his naval service.

TWO DIFFERENT VIEWS OF THE BIRCHES which stood off Birches Road where Meadow Vale is today. It was the home of the Gaskell family who had business interests in Liverpool and Birmingham and came to live in Codsall because of its good communications. They rented The Birches from the Wergs Hall Estate from 1901. The picture above shows Mrs Gaskell with her son Ernest, Holbrook Gaskell, Auntie Lily behind and William Smith, the gardener. The ensign flying (below) is a reminder of the shipping interests of the Gaskells.

SERVANTS AT THE BIRCHES around 1907. From left to right, back row: William Smith, gardener; Fanny Robinson, parlour maid; David Rostance, cowman; Sarah Pitt, housemaid; Walter Worskett, coachman; Ruth Shelton, kitchen maid; Charlie Thomas, groom. Front row: Clara Roberts, cook; Louisa Toye, housekeeper, and Morris the nurse holding Ernest.

THE GASKELL FAMILY. Frank Gaskell with his second wife Eva. Ernest is the older of the two boys, born in 1902. Roger his brother was born in 1915.

PENDRELL HALL around 1912. The Gaskells moved here from The Birches in 1910. The boy in the grounds is Ernest Gaskell. The hall was originally called Pendryl and was built in 1870 for Edward Viles of Bilston, editor of the *Gentlewoman's Journal*. Frank Gaskell remodelled the house and had the lodge built. In 1955 it was sold to Staffordshire County Council and is now in use as a residential college. Ernest Gaskell moved to Wood Hall and Roger to Wheatstone Park.

THE BILLIARD ROOM AT PENDRELL HALL. Although the large collection of oil paintings has now gone, the room is much the same today and is used as the dining room.

SERVANTS AT PENDRELL. From left to right, inside staff: scullery maid; upper housemaid; lower housemaid; Ada Walkington, Mrs Gaskell's maid; Rhoda Alice Neale, the cook; Rogers, the nanny; Kate the parlour maid. Outside staff: John Bright, gardener; George Picken, horse wagoner; Henry Roberts, cowman; Jack Barley, chauffeur; William Smith, gardener; Walter Worskett, coachman; Jack Leek, gardener; old Tom Bright; Beamond, estate manager.

THE CODSALL SECTION OF THE WOLVERHAMPTON VOLUNTEER DEFENCE FORCE during the First World War. They are outside The Firs in Wood Road which was built in the 1840s. Among the group are (back row) Jim Stevenson, Albert Richards, Harry Wilkes, Harris, Johnny Red-head, Alf Booth, (middle row) Jim Wall, Dick Alcock (far right).

CODSALL FIRE SERVICE during the Second World War at Oaken Terrace. The firemen are, from left to right: Maisie Burd, M. Sharples, Leading Fireman Bickley, Olwen Beech and Joan Beech.

CODSALL HOME GUARD during the Second World War, outside the Gun Room which stood in Wood Road, where the laundrette is now. From left to right: Tom Millington (postman), -?-, Harry Evans (Codsall Supply), Eric Evans, Ken Jones(?), Stan Illidge.

CODSALL CHURCH OF ENGLAND SCHOOL, Infants class 1919. The teacher is Edith Cockerill. She started at the school as a pupil in 1885, becoming a pupil teacher ten years later. She spent her whole teaching career there until her retirement in 1935 and was later Chairman of the Managers. Her memories of the school and area have been published locally. She died in 1983 aged 102.

STAFF OF CODSALL SECONDARY SCHOOL in the 1950s. From left to right, back row: C. Hill, A. Bould, G. Millington, J. Mansell, A. Sweeton, A. Robinson. Middle row: H. Porteous, E. McDonnel, N. Till, J. Kingscote, D. Williams, J. Palmer, H. Morton, M. Orton. Front row: Mr Burford, A. Wright, G. Gibbs (headteacher), E. Devey, Mr Franks. The school opened in 1940 and was extended in the '50s. It is now Codsall High School.

A FIRST YEAR CLASS at the Secondary school in 1953. The teacher is Mr Carroll.

A COLLECTION OF VEGETABLES FOR THE NAVY during the First World War at the rear of Woodfield. One of the ladies is Mrs Hazeldine who lived there at the time.

THE VICARAGE in 1951 after it had been reduced in size. It was built in 1848 and sold in 1979, a new vicarage having been built in the garden. The vicar is Revd Spinney, on his right is the architect. On his left is Mr Burd, the builder, and Roger Gaskell.

LANE GREEN, BILBROOK, before the building of the estate in the 1930s. The houses were built to accommodate workers from Boulton Paul's aircraft factory when the firm moved from Ipswich in 1936. A brochure was produced to illustrate the advantages of life 'amid unspoilt woodland scenery'. The estate was built by William Withers of Bilston and was also aimed at people living in Wolverhampton. House prices varied between £310 and £700. Shops, including the chemists, were built at the same time. The estate comprises Homefield Road, Withers Road and Florence Road. The Woodman can be seen on the left.

THE CHURCH OF THE HOLY CROSS. This photograph is taken from the booklet described above and shows the church before it was extended.

THE CHURCH OF THE HOLY CROSS after it had been extended in 1951 in memory of Lt.-Col. H.E. Twentyman of Bilbrook Manor. The church was built in 1898 and designed by F.T. Beck of Wolverhampton. It was extended again in 1965 and the bellcote was moved to the new east end. It came under Tettenhall parish until 1959.

BILBROOK MANOR HOUSE which stood off Bilbrook Road where Manor House Park is now. The house was known by this name by the 1880s. It was bought by Lt.-Col. Twentyman in the early 1900s and was demolished after his death in 1945.

THE TWENTYMAN BROTHERS outside the manor house around 1920. John Anthony, known as Tony, is on the left. He became a famous sculptor and died recently in Claverley. Richard was an architect. They are sitting on an AJS motorbike manufactured in Wolverhampton.

THE WOODMAN INN, 1935. The cows are grazing on the remains of the village green that gave Lane Green its name. William Hardware kept a beerhouse in Bilbrook in 1834; by 1851 he is listed as licensee of The Woodman inn. The proprietor in 1935 was Sam Gibson.

THE COTTAGE which stands on the bend in Bilbrook Road in the days when there were no other buildings around it except for the manor house whose wall can be seen on the left.

Codsall Wood, Oaken and Kingswood

THE FOAMING JUG, which stands on the Holyhead Road at the junction with Strawmoor Lane, in 1935 when it was kept by Mr and Mrs George Rowley. It was an inn by the 1880s having been converted from a private house.

OAKEN DRIVE with the lodge known locally as the Witches' Cottage. The drive once connected Codsall and Oaken and gave vehicular access to two large houses which still stand: Springfield House and Oaken Terrace. The central section is now merely a footpath. The cottage was the lower lodge to Springfield House and dates from around 1850.

HOLLYBUSH FARM COTTAGES, Hollybush Lane, which were provided for workers on the Wrottesley Estate. Behind them the Dower House can just be seen. Originally known as Oaken House it housed Belgian refugees during the First World War.

OAKEN VILLAGE in 1962. A row of three modern houses now stands on the left in place of the building which is end on to the road and was once the smithy. The post office pictured had been on this site since 1907.

TERRACE COTTAGES which stand opposite the former post office. The cottages were smaller then and had a communal washhouse and bakery at one end. They were used as accommodation for people who worked at the Terrace.

SHOP LANE in 1934. The houses on the left were originally council houses and were built in the early 1920s. On the right is a terrace of four cottages that was demolished in the sixties to make way for modern bungalows.

A RURAL SCENE, once typical of this area, taken off Stafford Lane.

CELEBRATIONS for the coronation of Queen Elizabeth II in 1953 in oaken village.

OAKEN MIXED HOCKEY CLUB in 1927. From left to right, standing: Jim Dumbell, Sibyl Hoole, Mary Parker, Pippen Burd, Audrey Hoole, Joy Thompson, Paul French, Ernest Gaskell. Sitting: Ian Walker, Kitty Elwell, Maisie Burd, Kathleen Hoole, ? Hoole.

CODSALL WOOD from the tower of Pendrell Hall.

AN AERIAL VIEW OF CODSALL WOOD in 1930. The Crown can be seen on the left on the corner of Whitehouse Lane.

LOOKING INTO CODSALL WOOD from the Pendrell side. The cottages on the left were originally opposite Pendrell Hall, but Frank Gaskell had them moved to their present location stone by stone. The cottage on the right was Tom Bright's.

CODSALL WOOD AND NEARBY CHILLINGTON HALL were a centre for excursions from nearby towns in the early 1900s. The lady is standing in front of a sign saying 'Teas Provided Good Stabling'. The building is still there, as are the cottages in the foreground. The cottage on the roadside has just been demolished. The Cross Guns' sign can be seen among the trees, proprietor C.J. Day.

THE CROWN INN with a good clear advertisement giving the proprietor as Aaron Martin. This dates it to around 1896. The trade directories describe him as a beerseller and do not mention the Crown by name. The earliest beerseller mentioned is Joseph Sale in 1834 who may also have kept the Crown.

THE JUNCTION INN, KINGSWOOD. Although it is still there, this building looks very different today. It now contains a wine bar. The lady in the doorway is Mrs Lillee and the licensee was J. Griffiths. The first mention of the Junction is in 1888.

KINGSWOOD COMMON, although smaller now than it was originally, is still used for picnics and the scenery has remained unchanged for a very long time. The mission church of St John the Baptist was built here in 1861 and a school added around 1874.

KINGSWOOD CAMP in the 1930s. This was a residential camp where schoolchildren from Wolverhampton were brought in order that they might enjoy the surrounding countryside. Accommodation was provided in wooden huts. In 1942 the Education Committee rented the camp and started a residential school for delicate children. Classrooms were built in 1954 and new residential buildings opened in 1960 enabling the school to become full-time.

STAFF OF KINGSWOOD SCHOOL. The headmaster, seated left, was Mr Frank MacMillan. Back row: Mr Thorpe, Ivy Howells, David Beech. Seated on the right is Nurse N.E. Beech. Front row: Mrs Marion MacMillan, Audrey Powell, Mrs Margaret Dorset, the cook.

THE SCHOOL WAS RUN AS AN OPEN AIR SCHOOL with as many lessons taken in the grounds as possible. Mr MacMillan is taking a junior class.

OUTDOOR ACTIVITIES WERE ENCOURAGED. These children have been on a nature ramble along lanes near the school. Wolverhampton Council still maintains an infants' centre at Kingswood.

ACKNOWLEDGEMENTS

The photographs for this volume have come from two main sources; Wolverhampton Public Libraries and Codsall Civic Society.

Wolverhampton Libraries and the author are grateful to the following people who have donated photographs to their collection either in the past or specially for this book and given permission for their use:

Aerofilms • Mr D. Bate • Mr Alex Chatwin • Mr Cecil Cox • Mr P. Eisenhofer
Express and *Star* • Mr C.R. Farmer • Mr Gabb • Mrs Faye Jones
Mr J. P. Jones • Mrs J. Holmes • Mr Alex MacMillan • Mrs Joyce Morris
Princess Irene Brigade Museum, Holland • Mrs D. Rogers • Mr David Rogers
Mrs M. Roper • Mrs Rushworth • Mr J. Russell • Mr Slater • Stafford Record
Office • Mrs Stait • Mrs Ann Tuck • William Salt Library • Mr Ned Williams
Mr D. Wilson • Mrs Wylde.

The author wishes to thank Codsall Civic Society for their co-operation in the preparation of the book. Special thanks must go to David Holden who has put together the society's large collection and given the author both time and information. The following people have loaned photographs to David Holden and given permission for them to be included:

Misses M. and P. Burd • Centra Heat • Mr Duckers • Mrs Gladys Evans
The Gaskell Family • Mr and Mrs Hookway • Mrs Illidge • Mr David McGeoch
Mrs Hilda Porteous • Mr Ray Powell • Mrs Ray • Mrs Vera Taylor.

The author also wishes to thank the following people for donations of photographs and for information:

Mr John Blamire Brown • Mrs S. Baynham • Mrs D. Dalton • Mr Alan Hughes
Miss Angela Tonks • Mr Maurice Wheeler • Mrs Wills.

Apologies must go to anybody whose name has been unwittingly missed from the list of donations.